C000064995

OSAKA

by Hoikusha Publishing
Co., Ltd.

translated by
Thomas I. Elliott

HOIKUSHA
保育社

CONTENTS

OSAKA

KINKI DISTRICT

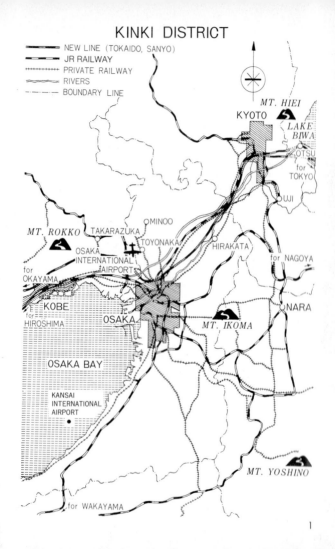

NEW LINE (TOKAIDO, SANYO)
JR RAILWAY
PRIVATE RAILWAY
RIVERS
BOUNDARY LINE

MT. HIEI
KYOTO
LAKE BIWA
OTSU
for TOKYO
UJI
OMINOO
TAKARAZUKA
TOYONAKA
HIRAKATA
MT. ROKKO
for NAGOYA
OSAKA INTERNATIONAL AIRPORT
for OKAYAMA
KOBE
for HIROSHIMA
OSAKA
MT. IKOMA
NARA
OSAKA BAY
KANSAI INTERNATIONAL AIRPORT
MT. YOSHINO
for WAKAYAMA

1

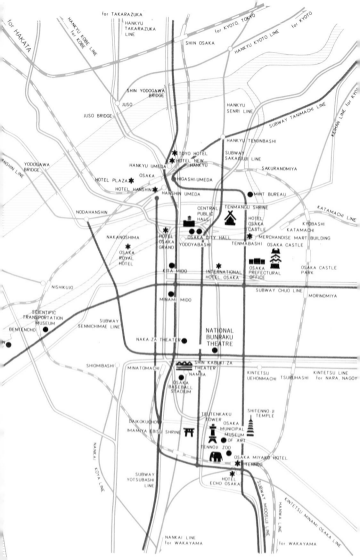

OSAKA

translated by Thomas I. Elliott

© All rights reserved. No.19 of Hoikusha's Color Books Series.Published by Hoikusha Publishing Co., Ltd., 8-6, 4-chome, Tsurumi, Tsurumi-ku, Osaka,538 Japan. ISBN 4-586-54019-2. First Edition in 1970. 12th Edition in 1996. Printed in JAPAN

Bird's-eye view of Shin Osaka Station area

3

The Shinkansen

Shin Osaka Station

Shin Osaka Station

The New Tokaido Line was completed in 1963 to connect Osaka and Tokyo. The fastest expresses, the "bullet-trains," race from Shin Osaka Station to Tokyo Station at speeds up to 130 m.p.h. The station area was once rice paddies. Today, its entire character has been urbanized to fit it for new roles in business, tourism, and industry. This line was extended to Hakata, Kyushu in 1975.

Pedestrian overpass in front of Osaka Station: convenient, and safe from the heavy traffic below

Kansai International Airport

Kansai International Airport

On September 4, 1994 there came up on the sea of Osaka Bay, 5 kilometer off the shore of the southeastern part of Osaka, a magnificent international air-port which is, for the first time in japan, fully equipped for around-the-clock operation. The future development of this new airport is expected to become a hub airport. of the world which annually will handle 32 million passengers and 1.1 million tons of cargo and will make 160 thousand times of taking off and landing available.

Passenger Terminal Building of Kansai International Airport

Passenger Terminal Building, inside

The Downtown
Expressway
winds its way
above Osaka's
crowded streets.

11

A building-tunnel for Osaka's Downtown Expressway

Downtown Expressway

This three-lane (partly four-lane), one-way Expressway runs a complete circle around Osaka. The Downtown Expressway connects to the Meishin Expressway for either Kobe or Nagoya, to Kinki Highway, Chugoku Highway, and to the suburbs. A drive around the Expressway affords a fine tour of the city.

12

Scientific Transportation Museum

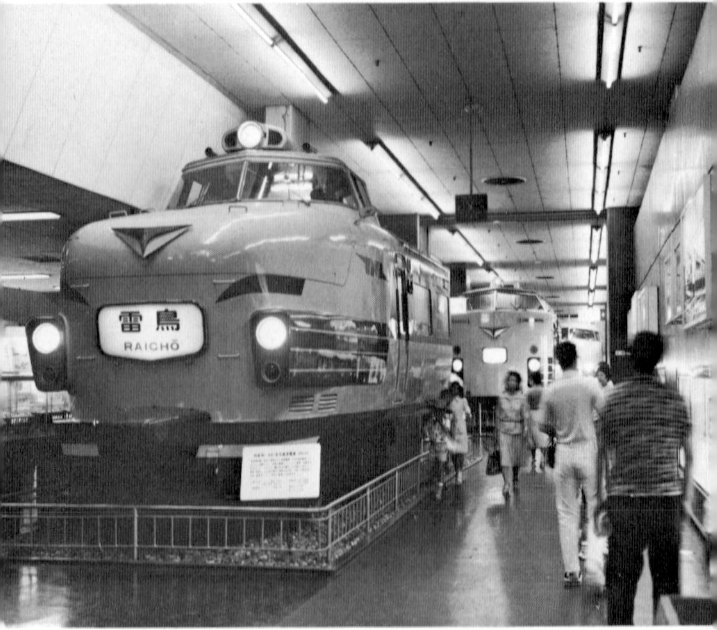

The Tower of Osaka Castle is seen in foreground. It was first built by Toyotomi Hideyoshi in the 16th century and rebuilt in 1931 by the citizens of Osaka. The complex of buildings seen in

the distance is called OBP. (Osaka Business Park). The buildings, Twin 21, Crystal Tower, Matsushita IMP Building etc., constitute a hub of information and culture.

Osaka Harbor
Container Terminal

Osaka Nanko with its container terminal is a foreign trade port where annually 1,414 container ships with gross tonnage of 33.07 million are sailing in and out in service for mainly North American, North European, Mediterranean and Australian routes. According to 1994 official statistics the total handling quantity of containerized goods at Osaka Harbor is 13.2 million tons of which the goods handled at South Port Container Terminal occupy 8.73 million tons.

On the other hand, Public Container Terminal equipped at present with six berths is in operation and especially Berth c-9 with large-sized crane and the depth of 13 meters can deal with big sized ships.

Container Terminal

Ferry Terminal

Ferry Terminal

International Ferry Terminal is at present located at Wharf K of Sakishima (Nanko). Ferry which connects Osaka to Shanghai originates here and handles 7,700 passengers and about 136 thousand tons of cargo annually. Another new international ferry terminal is now under construction at a corner of Cosmo Square.

Tenpozan Passenger Boat Terminal is nicely equipped as an exclusive terminal for overseas tourist boats, and many gorgeous passenger boats of round-the-world cruise call at this Terminal.

Fishing at Kema Dam

◀ Yodo River at dusk

Toyosato Bridge: it is somehow sad to see a modern bridge replacing the little boats that ferried people across the Yodo River.

Yodo River

The Yodo River flows fifty miles from Lake Biwa, Japan's largest lake, to empty in Osaka Bay. It divides into several smaller rivers after entering Osaka. The Yodo River has contributed for centuries to Osaka's growth.

Section of the "Yodo River" scroll by Okyo Maruyama

Wood-block print by Hiroshige

21

Pots of flowers decorate Yodoya Bridge.

Bridges

Osaka is known as a city of water, and a city of bridges. Some bridges are long, some short; some seem strangely placed, others have interesting shapes and designs. Large and small included, there are over 1,500 bridges in the city.

Roaring lion guards Naniwa Bridge's approach.

The Expressway cuts across Korai Bridge.

Juso Bridge: the most congested of the many bridges fording the Yodo River

Nakanoshima's small bridge

Sakura-no-Miya Bridge, near the Mint Bureau; its silver
paint causes the popular appendage Silver Bridge.

Osaka Bay Bridge (Minato-Ohashi)

Japan's Mint Bureau: the refined Senpu-kan, Osaka's oldest western-style building

Cherry-blossom viewing on ▶ Mint Bureau grounds

Mint Bureau

Japan's Mint Bureau is the only major government office in Osaka. It was constructed in 1871, following the unification of Japan's monetary system. Today, all of Japan's coin money is minted here. The western-style Senpukan Hall was built as a reception house. The mint grounds are closed to the public except for a short period in April each year. The grounds are opened then to permit the people to view the Mint's famous double cherry blossoms.

Mint Bureau

Coin minting machine

Attendants check 500 coins per minute

Gingko trees line Midosuji Boulevard

◄ Midosuji Boulevard, Osaka's main thoroughfare, connects Osaka Station and the Namba area

31

Midosuji Boulevard

Osaka's main thoroughfare. 145 feet wide and almost three miles long, Midosuji Boulevard runs straight northsouth from Osaka Station, crossing Yodoya Bridge, to Namba. Multi-storied buildings and rows of gingko trees line the Boulevard.

Shin Kabuki-za Theatre on Midosuji Boulevard; the architectural style originated in 16th century Japan

Midosuji Boulevard's Name derives from the Temples
called Kita Mido (above) and Minami Mido (below).

33

Osaka's New Transportation, Aqua Bus

Inside the Merchandise Mart Building

Bustling Dobuike,
a wholesalers' district

Osaka's Senba area undergoes a facelifting

Senba

An area with Honmachi as its center and lying midway between Umeda and Namba along Midosuji Boulevard has been and is called Senba. From old times Senba is well-known as Osaka's business center. Doshomachi, a wholesale district of pharmaceutical goods, and Dobuike, another district of textile wholesale business, are still keeping up the atmosphere of the past. The name Senba, literally "the place for ships," has a history that Hideyoshi Toyotomi, a shogun in the 16th century, made efficient use of ships as the fundamentals of economic prosperity.

Doshomachi, area
for pharmaceutical
wholesalers

Merchant's house reminiscent of old Senba

Central Public Hall on Nakanoshima

Nakanoshima Island

Osaka is likened to Paris due to its mid-city island. Besides many first-rate business firms, Nakanoshima boasts the Bank of Japan (Osaka branch), Osaka City Hall, Central Public Hall, Osaka Prefectural Library, and various other institutions and buildings. The eastern, upstream end of Nakanoshima is a public park.

◀ Nakanoshima Island, in the heart of the city

Osaka City Hall on Nakanoshima ; the light tower on rooftop houses a famous bell called "miotsukushi" (channel marks) bell.

◀ Festival Hall

Osaka Prefectural Library

Museum of Oriental Ceramics, Osaka

Osaka Castle's Tower bathed in light

Osaka Castle

More than any other structure in the city, Osaka Castle symbolizes Osaka. The castle was built in 1583 by Hideyoshi Toyotomi, and its history is truly Osaka's history. The present reinforced concrete Tower dates from 1931.

Turret overlooking the Osaka Castle▶
moat; Merchandise Mart Building in left
background

Great stone at Osaka Castle's Otemon Gate

Osaka Prefectural Office fronts on Osaka Castle's moat.

Remains of Naniwa Palace

Osaka Municipal Museum inside the gates of Osaka Castle

Umeda underground shopping center

Kita (Osaka Station Area)

Although there are many shopping districts in the city of Osaka , Kita (Osaka Station Area) and Minami (Namba Station Area) are the most typical shopping areas. Especially Kita is the most thriving town with modern office districts as Nakanoshima in its vicinity and having many department stores, specialty stores, hotels and restaurants in the area. There are also widely developed underground shopping centers in the this area which contend for the first place as underground shopping facilities in Japan.

◀ Osaka Station area

A man-made brook flows through Umeda Underground Shopping Area. The shopping promenade with fashionable stores along the brook attracts many shoppers and tourists.

Subways criss-cross under the city

The water fountain in the Umeda Underground Shopping Area

Shinsaibashi Bridge was not always a pedestrian overpass.

Shinsaibashisuji

Osaka's busiest shopping street, 25 feet wide and 2,500 feet long, Shinsaibashisuji runs between Shinsaibashi Bridge and Ebisubashi Bridge. Widely varied shops line both sides of the covered street. Some shops, as specialty stores, have been in one family for generations handling specific goods, while others sell more modern products through colorful window displays.

◀ Shinsaibashisuji, Osaka's busiest shopping area

Dotonbori

Attractive decorations make window shopping pleasant along Shinsaibashisuji.

Naka-za Theatre displays
a rare cupola with
a family crest on its
lower roof.

National Bunraku Theatre

Buddhist deities are remembered even near bustling amusement areas.

Minami (Namba Station Area)

Minami competes with the Osaka Station Area for shopping and entertainment. Minami includes the area around Namba Station, Sennichimae, and all the streets up to Shinsaibashi and the Dotonbori River.

◀Dotonbori amusement area, famous for food, theatre, and fun

Namba Station Area with Nankai South Tower Hotel in back

Nagai Natural History Museum

Osaka Science Museum

Utsubo Park

Shitennoji Temple's Golden Hall and Five-storied Pagoda

Shitennoji Temple

Constructed in 593 by order of Prince Shotoku, Shitennoji Temple ranks with Nara's Horyuji Temple as one of Japan's oldest. The temple was almost totally destroyed during the Second World War, and its present structures are postwar reinforced concrete buildings.

Paranirvana mural in the Five-storied Pagoda

Keitakuen: Japanese garden in Tennoji Park

Interior of Osaka Municipal
Museum of Art

Kurayashiki Gate near the Municipal Museum of Art was originally the Entrance to the Kuroda Clan's Warehouse

Looking north from Tsutenkaku Tower

Shinsekai

The Shinsekai area, originally known as Luna Park, was designed in the late 19th century to imitate New York's Coney Island. Tsutenkaku Tower was meant to copy Paris' Eiffel Tower. This is the most common of Osaka's various amusement quarters.

◀ Tsutenkaku Tower in the Shinsekai area

63

Tennoji Station

Tennoji Botanical Garden

Abeno Area

Tennoji Zoo

Portable shrines float down the
Dojima River by boat

Tenjin Festival

This festival held at Tenma Shrine, ranks
with Kyoto's Gion Festival and Tokyo's Kanda
Festival as one of Japan's three great festivals.
The Tenjin Festival , celebrated on July 24th
and 25th, reaches its climax when a fleet of
boats carries portable shrines down the Dojima
River.

66

Tenjin Festival, one of Japan's three great festivals

Sacred bamboo grass promising good fortune in the New Year is sold during the Toka-Ebisu Festival.

Toka Ebisu Festival

This festival of Imamiya Ebisu Shrine is traditionally popular among Osaka's merchant class. Ebisu is a Buddhist deity who promises good fortune for New Year. The festival is held for three days from January 9th to 11th.

Rice-planting Festival at Sumiyoshi Taisha Shrine

Shrine maidens in the precincts of
Sumiyoshi Taisha Shrine

Sumiyoshi Taisha Shrine

As a Shinto Shrine dedicated to sea
deities, it was originally erected next to the
water. Land reclamation has pushed the
water away until the shrine today stands
almost three miles inland. The Main Hall's
architectural style is peculiar to this shrine,
and is called Sumiyoshi-zukuri.

◀Sumiyoshi Taisha Shrine's arched bridge

Burial Mound of Emperor Nintoku — its 552,000
Square Yards makes it the World's Largest Tomb in area.

Osaka Prefectural University

Osaka Municipal University

Bunraku Puppet Performance — Handling
the puppets requires great skill
acquired through years of training.

Takarazuka

Takarazuka is famous above all for its Girls'
Opera. Many young girls from all over Japan and
also adult women, and even old chap fans
although a few, pay frequent visit to Takarazuka
Grand Theatre.

Takarazuka Troupe's total splendor at curtain call

Bunraku

The Bunraku Puppet drama originated and was brought to perfection in Osaka. It ranks with Kabuki and Noh in representing Japan's traditional drama. In Bunraku, a joruri ballad-drama is recited to the musical accompaniment of the shamisen.

Traditional Bugaku, court dance and music

Bunraku Puppet Heads — two young
girls and two male characters

77

Tenpozan
Tenpozan Bridge connecting
Nanko, a reclaimed land, to
the City mainland. The red
and blue colored building in
foreground is Kaiyukan (Osaka Aquarium).
A round building at the right
of Kaiyukan is Suntory Museum.

Kaiyukan Osaka Aquarium

Whale shark cared and exhibited in Kaiyukan

A tall rectangular building in the center
is WTC (Osaka World Trade Center).
ATC (Asia Pacific Trade Center) is seen on the left end.

Water Front

The wide area along the coast of Osaka Harbor is now being regenerated and remodelled by reclamation. The size of the total reclamation reaches 1,617 ha. Tenpozan Harbor Village and Cosmo Square on the reclaimed land are base spots of culture and recreation. Tenpozan Harbor Village comprises Kaiyukan Aquarium, Museum and Market Place. Cosmo Square is an artificial marine city with an area of 1,002 ha. There are high-rise apartment buildings where people are already settled in and other big buildings which are mostly cultural or commercial accomodations such as Intechs Osaka, Wine Museum. ATC (Asia Pacific Trade Center) and WTC (Osaka World Trade Center).

Evening Concert in Summer
at the Shopping Center

Senri New Town

There stretches a range of gentle hills called Senri Hills, in 10 km north from of Osaka. In 1970 Expo was held here and coincidently with it, the constrution of Senri New Town was taken place. The area of Senri New Town is about 1,160 ha and over 100,000 people are living there. Having decades passed since the inauguration of the town, it is now in the second stage of its development with a comfortable living environment of affluent verdure of grown-up trees and plants.

Apartment Complex in Senri New Town ▶

Minoo Park's famous waterfall

Hattori Park boasts of tennis courts, a baseball field, and playing fields for other sports.

Kansai University, near the Meishin Expressway

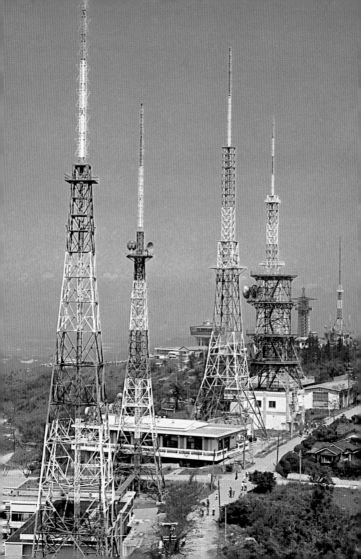

Million Dollar View — Kobe seen from Mount Rokko

Mounts Ikoma and Rokko

These two mountains form backdrops for Osaka and Kobe. Private railway lines and new expressways have brought them within an hour's ride from either city. Summer temperatures atop the mountains are ten to twenty degrees Fahrenheit cooler than in the city, making them popular retreats during hot spells.

◀ Television Towers atop Mount Ikoma

Hirakata Park attracts autumn crowds to view its chrysanthemum dolls.

Chairlift atop Mount Ikoma

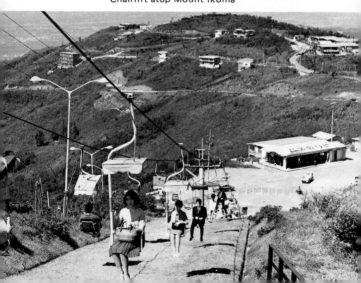

Shell-gathering (Tannowa)

Takarazuka Family Land, a short walk from
Takarazuka Station

Port Tower, symbol of Kobe Port

Kobe

Kobe is a beautiful city facing the sea and having mountains at the back. It is located about 30 kirometer west of Osaka. Kobe has many sightseeing spots, such as exotic shopping streets of Sannomiya, the Rokko mountains, seaside resort of Suma, a hot spa in Arima foreigner's mansions of Kitanocho district and Harbor Land which was recently developed on the seashore. Also, Port Island and Rokko Island which are artificial marine towns appearing on the water of Kobe Harbor are most unique places to visit.

(At 5:46 a.m. on January 17. 1995 a formidable earthquake of a magnitude of 7.2 happened near Kobe and the city suffered a heavy damage. The city is at present trying reconstruct itself with all its energies and efforts. The picture shown here is the one taken before the earthquake destroyed Kobe.)

Kobe City viewed from Port Tower

Kobe Trade Building and Expressway

Kobe City Hall on Sakaemachi Street

Rokko Golf Course

Sumaura Park Ropeway up Mount Hachibuse

The abstract Sun Tower. Its three faces represent the past, present, and future.

Expo Park

After Expo '70 was over, the site with an area of 2.64 million square meters was made into a park. It is an all-embracing grand park with EXPOLAND (an amusement park), Japanese Garden, National Museum of Ethnology, National Museum of Art, Osaka tennis courts, an archery field, a baseball field and a football field in it, and therefore it is a place of recreation and relaxation for the citizens. The abstract Sun Tower, which was the symbol of Expo '70, has been preserved in a state of perfection and it is now the symbol of Expo Park.

EXPOLAND for Children

National Museum of Ethnology in EXPO '70 Site

Japanese garden in EXPO '70 Site

CONTENTS

LOCATION

Osaka City, the seat of Osaka Prefectural government, is bounded on the west by Osaka Bay, and on the three other sides by mountains. North is the Tamba region, east are Mounts Ikoma and Kongo, and south is the Izumi Range. The Yodo River, the Yamato River, the Muko River and others, flow through the area to empty in Osaka Bay. The region's climate is generally temperate.

North of Osaka City are Suita, Ibaraki, and Takatsuki, centers of heavy and petrochemicals, electrical machinery, and food processing industries. To the east are Moriguchi, Yao, and Higashi Osaka, centers of steel and machine manufacturing industries. Sakai to the south is also a steel center, while Izumi Otsu, Kishiwada, and Kaizuka are textile centers. The general area around Senri Hills in Suita is residential. Other nearby cities, from which large segments of Osaka's working population commute, include Minoo, Ikeda, Toyonaka, Hirakata.

HISTORIC BACKGROUND

Japan's two main areas are Kanto and Kansai. Tokyo and Yokohama are the largest cities in the former area. The latter includes Osaka, Kyoto and Kobe. While Tokyo is the political capital, Osaka has long been Japan's commercial capital. Osaka first began acquiring its commercial nature in the fifteenth century.

Ancient Japan developed primarily in the areas known today as Nara, Kyoto and Osaka. Japan's historic capitals and largest cities were located in these areas, and in northern Kyushu. Accessibility was not the primary reason for choosing a site in days of constant civil strife, a fact which partly explains why Kyoto, inaccessible by water and surrounded on three sides by mountains, remained the capital for almost eleven hundred years.

The Osaka area was called Naniwa in ancient Japan, and was the capital for short intervals during the Yamato Period — the middle seventh, and the early eighth centuries. Passage to the Asian mainland was possible from Naniwa through the Seto Inland Sea. In medieval Japan, Naniwa became Sakai — the precursor of modern-day Osaka.

Osaka's urbanization gained its initial impetus in 1496 when Rennyo (1415-1499), hereditary head of the powerful Shinshu sect Honganji Temple in Kyoto, built another Honganji Temple as a great religious fortress in Osaka. The Shinshu sect's soldier-monks were defeated and Osaka's Honganji Temple was destroyed by Oda Nobunaga in 1580. Toyotomi Hideyoshi later built Osaka Castle on the same site. He invited merchants from Sakai, Fushimi, Hirano, and other areas to settle around the castle, and the town began to flourish. Hostilities between

Hideyoshi and the Tokugawa forces destroyed the town on two occasions, but both times it survived to recover its former prosperity. When feudal clans from western Japan opened commercial offices and warehouses in Osaka in the early 17 century, Osaka suddenly expanded rapidly. By the Meiji Restoration in 1868, Osaka was so prosperous that some factions advocated locating Japan's new capital there rather than in Edo.

By 1940 Osaka was a great metropolis with a population of almost three million people. World War II, however, levelled one-third of the city. Osaka struggled to regain its former economic status in the postwar period, and in the process the entire area acquired an industrial character. Heavy and petrochemicals, ship-building, electric equipment manufacturing, food processing, machine manufacturing, steel, and other industries all sprouted rapidly.

TRAVEL TO OSAKA

Visitors to Osaka will at first arrive at one of the following spots:

I. by air; Kansai International Airport or
          Osaka International Airport
II. by railway JR; Shin-Osaka Station or Osaka Station
III. by car; Suita Interchange or Toyonaka Interchange of
          Meishin Expressway or Suita Interchange of
          Chugoku Expressway

■From the spot the city of Osaka is within easy access by:

I. Arriving by airplane

●Limousine Bus

●Railroad

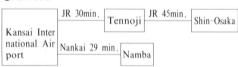

II. Arriving by railway

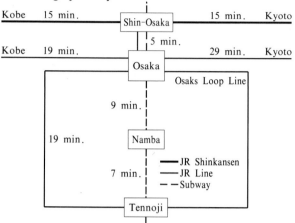

Kobe   15 min.   [Shin-Osaka]   15 min.   Kyoto

Kobe   19 min.   5 min.   29 min.   Kyoto

[Osaka]

Osaks Loop Line

9 min.

19 min.   [Namba]

7 min.   ━ JR Shinkansen
── JR Line
┈ Subway

[Tennoji]

III. Arriving by car

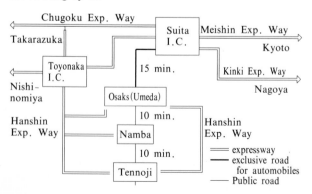

Chugoku Exp. Way   [Suita I.C.]   Meishin Exp. Way

Takarazuka   Kyoto

[Toyonaka I.C.]   15 min.   Kinki Exp. Way

Nishi-nomiya   Nagoya

[Osaks (Umeda)]

Hanshin Exp. Way   10 min.   Hanshin Exp. Way

[Namba]   ═ expressway
━ exclusive road
   for automobiles
── Public road

10 min.

[Tennoji]

SIGHTSEEING

Though a historic city, Osaka cannot compete in tourist attractions with old religious and political centers like Kyoto and Nara. Except for the Shitennoji Temple, Osaka Castle, Sumiyoshi Taisha Shrine, Emperor Nintoku's Tomb, and the Naniwa Palace site, Osaka's sightseeing spots are fairly modern. Many relate to the city's commercial role in the Japanese economy.

The contemporary folkways and arts of Osaka are mostly inheritances dating from the late twelfth to the middle nineteenth centuries. Japanese theatre arts like Bunraku and Kamigata Kabuki could not have developed anywhere but in Osaka.

Tourist information service is available at the Central Information Booths in Shin Osaka, Osaka, and Tennoji stations, and at all offices of the Japan Travel Bureau (JTB).

1. Osaka castle:10-minute walk from Otemae bus stop
2. Shitennoji Temple 5-minute walk from Saimon-mae bus or Shitennoji-mae subway stop (Tanimachi Line)
3. Sumiyoshi Taisha Shrine:10-minute walk from Sumiyoshi Taisha on the main Nankai Line
4. Mint Bureau: Bus from Sakuranomiya on the Loop Line
5. Osaka Port: Bus or Chuo Line subway direct to Osaka Port
6. Nakanoshima: Yodoyabashi on the Midosuji Line subway and Keihan Line; Kitahama on the Sakaisuji Line subway and Keihan Line; Higobashi on the Yotsubashi Line subway; bus to Tenjinbashi, Kitahama, or Oebashi
7. Merchandise Mart Building: Tenmabashi on the Tanimachi Line subway and Keihan Line; bus to Tenmabashi
8. Shinsaibashi: Shinsaibashi on the Midosuji Line subway; bus to Shinsaibashi

9. National Bunraku Theatre: Nipponbashi on the Sakaisuji and Sennichimae Lines subway; bus to Dotonbori
10. Shinsekai: Dobutsuen-mae on the Midosuji Line subway and Ebisu-cho on the Sakaisuji Line
11. Festival Hall: Higobashi on the Yotsubashi Line subway; bus to Higobashi
12. International Trade Fair Exhibition Hall: Bentencho on the Chuo Line subway and Loop Line
13. Mount Rokko: bus from Rokko on the Hankyu Line; also accessible by car
14. Mount Ikoma: cable car from Ikoma on the Kintetsu Line; also accessible by car
15. Hattori Park: Hattori on the Hankyu Line
16. Minoo Park: Minoo on the Hankyu Line

Nakanoshima Park

17. Hirakata Park: Hirakata Koen on the Keihan Line
18. Tannowa Park: Tannowa on the main Nankai Line
19. Takarazuka: Takarazuka on the Hankyu Line

Athletic Fields

Nissei Baseball Stadium: Subway or Loop Line to Morino-
miya
Municipal Central Gymnasium: Subway to Tanimachi
Yonchome
Nagai Track and Field Stadium: Subway to Nagai
Hanazono Rugby Field: Hanazono on the Kintetsu-Nara
Line

Department Store

Daimaru: Umeda Branch-Central Exit Osaka Station;
Shinsaibashi Branch-Midosuji Line subway to
Shinsaibashi
Hankyu: East Exit Osaka Station
Hanshin: Central Exit Osaka Station
Kintetsu: Abeno Branch – Tennoji subway stop, Ueroku
Branch – Uehonmachi on the Kintetsu Line
Matsuzakaya: Tanimachi Line subway or Keihan Line to
Tenmabashi
Mitsukoshi: Kitahama on the Keihan Line and Sakaisuji
Line subway
Sogo: Midosuji Line subway to Shinsaibashi
Takashimaya: Midosuji Line subway to Namba, or Namba
on the Nankai Line

Tours on the Double Decker Sightseeing Bus
"Niji" (Rainbow)

	Tour	Starting Time	Fare Adult Child
A	Castle & Aqua Bus Tour	Mon. ~ Fri. 10:00 Sat. & Sun. 14:00	¥4,100 ¥1,950
D	Castle and Tsutenkaku Tower Tour	Mon. ~ Fri. 14:00	¥2,920 ¥1,270
K2	Museum & Japanese Garden Tour	Sat. & Sun. of June~ 9:30 Aug., Dec. Jan.	¥3,770 ¥1,590
C	Castle, Shrines and Temple Tour	everyday 9:10	¥2,810 ¥1,280
K1	Castle and Flower Garden Tour	Sat. & Sun. of Feb. ~May and 10:30 Sep. ~Nov.	¥3,170 ¥1,280
L	Aquarium and Sumiyoshi Taisha Tour	everyday 14:30 (no tour when Kaiyukan is closed)	¥4,220 ¥2,130

■Boarding Osaka Station Midosuji Exit M: P.8(B-2).
  For inquiries and other questions call the Umeda
  (Osaka Station) Sightseeing Bus Station
  Tel. 06-311-2995

Osaka Boat Tour (please call to confirm departure times)

Cruise	Course	Fare Adult Child
Bayline (Osaka Port Tour)	Tour course from Oaka Port Central Pier into the Yodogawa and Yamatogawa Rivers.	¥820 ¥410
Aqua-Liner (Water Tour Buses)	From Osaka Castle Port, Temmabashi Port and Yodoyabashi Port. 60 minutes time required.	¥1,800 ¥900
Santa Maria (Tempozan Bay Tour)	From Tempozan to the Bay Area ■For inquiries and other questions call the Osaka Aqua Bus Co., Ltd. (942-5511)	Day Cruise ¥1,500 ¥ 750 Night Cruise ¥2,750 ¥1,380

HOTEL GUIDE

Japan's western style hotels enjoy a fine reputation among world travellers for good service, congenial atmosphere, and outstanding accommodations.

The following list is of hotels in Osaka, Kyoto, Kobe, Nara, Otsu, and Takarazuka, The adventuresome individual who wants to experience the Japanese inn (*ryokan*) should consult his travel agent.

Osaka Royal Hotel

Hotel Plaza

LIST OF HOTELS

OSAKA

Hotel Granvia Osaka	Tel. (06) 344-1235
The Westin Osaka	Tel. (06) 440-1111
ANA Sheraton Hotel, Osaka	Tel. (06) 347-1112
Osaka Grand Hotel	Tel. (06) 202-1212
International Hotel Osaka	Tel. (06) 941-2661
Osaka Royal Hotel	Tel. (06) 448-1121
Osaka Hilton Hotel	Tel. (06) 347-7111
Hotel New Otani, Osaka	Tel. (06) 941-1111
Hotel Hankyu International	Tel. (06) 377-21
Hotel New Hankyu	Tel. (06) 372-5101
Toyo Hotel	Tel. (06) 372-8181
Hotel Hanshin	Tel. (06) 344-1661
Hotel Plaza	Tel. (06) 453-1111
Osaka Castle Hotel	Tel. (06) 942-2401
Tennoji Miyako Hotel	Tel. (06) 779-1501
Nankai South Tower Hotel	Tel. (06) 646-1111
Hotel Nikko, Osaka	Tel. (06) 244-1111
Miyako Hotel, Osaka	Tel. (06) 773-1111

KOBE

Kobe Portpia Hotel	Tel. (078) 302-1111
Oriental Hotel	Tel. (078) 331-8111
Rokko Oriental Hotel	Tel. (078) 891-0333
Rokkosan Hotel	Tel. (078) 891-0301

TAKARAZUKA

Takarazuka Hotel	Tel. (0797) 87-1151

Oriental Hotel

Hotel Fujita Kyoto

KYOTO

Hotel Fujita Kyoto	Tel. (075) 222-1511
Kyoto Grand Hotel	Tel. (075) 341-2311
Kyoto International Hotel	Tel. (075) 222-1111
Kyoto Hotel	Tel. (075) 211-5111
Miyako Hotel	Tel. (075) 771-7111
Hotel New Kyoto	Tel. (075) 801-2111
Hotel Sunflower Kyoto	Tel. (075) 761-9111
Kyoto Palaceside Hotel	Tel. (075) 431-8171
Kyoto Prince Hotel	Tel. (075) 781-4141

Kyoto Takaragaike Prince Hotel	Tel. (075) 712-1111
Kyoto Royal Hotel	Tel. (075) 223-1234
Kyoto Station Hotel	Tel. (075) 361-7151
Kyoto Tower Hotel	Tel. (075) 361-3211
Hotel The Mount Hiei	Tel. (075) 701-2111

NARA

Nara Hotel	Tel. (0742) 26-3300

Miyako Hotel

Kyoto Hotel

RESTAURANT GUIDE

Here we will introduce only a few of the great many restaurants in Osaka, Kyoto and Kobe. The establishments listed, however, are guaranteed to provide you with first-class service, cuisine and atmosphere. Restaurants are categorized by city and cuisine served. Short notes are appended when appropriate to mention a house specialty. Telephone numbers and simple directions have been provided. Directions in Japanese may be shown a taxi driver. Some restaurants require advance reservations.

Osaka, Kobe and Kyoto each has its own gastronomic peculiarities. Osakans are known throughout Japan as fussy eaters, and pride themselves on being connoisseurs of fine food. Many excellent restaurants exist in Osaka to cater to their taste. Kobe, on the other hand, is Japan's busiest port town, and boasts of a large and diverse foreign population. The community's international flavor finds expression in the exotic and authentic cuisines available. Foreigners from the particular country often manage Italian, Indian and other ethnic restaurants. Kyoto, meanwhile, frequently called the spiritual home of all Japanese, was Japan's capital for eleven hundred years. This contributed to making Kyotoites conservative and highly tradition-conscious. At the same time, however, Kyoto is one of Japan's most colorful tourist attractions. These two aspects of Kyoto's nature appear in the shops serving traditional Kyoto-style Japanese food, and the western restaurants catering to Japanese and foreign tourists.

Four Japanese dishes are *tempura, sukiyaki, sushi,* and *kaiseki ryori.* Foreigners generally consider *tempura* the closest to western food. The Portugese supposedly introduced it to

Japan in the sixteenth century, and by 1700 it was being prepared in common Japanese households. Fresh fish, shellfish, and vegetables are dipped in flour and egg, and fried in boiling oil. Preferably, *tempura* is eaten hot after dipping in a special sauce.

Sukiyaki may be the best-known Japanese food. Thinly cut beef is cooked together with various vegetables in a frying pan set on a table. Sugar and soy sauce and *sake* are added to the cooking mixture. Guests seated around the table eat the *sukiyaki* as it is cooked. It is usually dipped in a beaten raw egg that may be flavored with soy sauce.

Sushi, which used to be unjustly underrated by foreigners as one of the infamous raw fish dishes Japanese eat, has nowadays become one of the most famous Japanese dishes particularly popular among American. European and Australian people. Four styles of *sushi* are *nigirizushi, makizushi, oshizushi,* and *chirashizushi.*

Kaiseki Ryori is a pure Japanese cuisine. At the zenith of the popularity of the tea ceremony in the fifteenth century, food was served at tea gatherings. The food eventually became a meal which grew increasingly lavish until it broke from the tea ceremony to become an independent ritual. That meal is today's *kaiseki ryori.* Generally, much drinking accompanys the meal. It is frequently the service style for formal parties or ceremonious occasions.

RESTAURANTS

≪Kaiseki Ryori≫

Kagairo
   1,Kitahama,Chuo-ku   Tel.(06)231-7214

Kitcho
   3,Koraibashi,Chuo-ku   Tel.(06)231-1937

Sakau
   4,Hirano-machi,Chuo-ku   Tel.(06)231-2225

Tsuruya
   4,Imabashi,Chuo-ku   Tel.(06)231-0456

Yamatoya
   Soemon-cho,Chuo-ku   Tel.(06)211-0058

Ikuo
   8,Kakuda-cho,Kita-ku   Tel.(06)315-7738

Kigawa
   1,Dotonbori,Chuo-ku   Tel.(06)211-3030

≪Sukiyaki≫

Honmiyake
   3,Nakanoshima,Kita-ku   Tel.(06)231-3188

Hariju
   1,Dotonbori,Chuo-ku   Tel.(06)211-7777

Edogiku
   2,Kawara-machi,Chuo-ku   Tel.(06)231-5858

Kitamura
   1,Higashi-shinsaibashi,Chuo-ku   Tel.(06)245-4129

≪Tempura≫

Kitahachi
   2,Imabashi,Chuo-ku   Tel.(06)231-0267

Ippou
   8,Kakuda-cho,Kita-ku   Tel.(06)361-3828
Tenkichi
   3,Namba,Chuo-ku   Tel.(06)641-6166

≪Unagi≫
Chikuyotei
   Nakanoshima,Kita-ku   Tel.(06)441-1883
Honkeshibato
   3,Awaji-cho,Chuo-ku   Tel.(06)231-4819
Gencho
   3,Dosho-machi,Chuo-ku   Tel.(06)231-0344
Hishito
   5,Fukushima,Fukushima-ku   Tel.(06)451-5094

≪Sushi≫
Sushiman
   4,Koraibashi,Chuo-ku   Tel.(06)231-1520
Yoshinozushi
   3,Awaji-cho,Chuo-ku   Tel.(06)231-7181
Honfukuzushi
   Shinsaibashi-suji   Chuo-ku   Tel.(06)271-3344
Kamezushi
   Sonezaki,Kita-ku   Tel.(06)312-3862
Sushimasa
   2,Sonezaki,Kita-ku   Tel.(06)361-1743

≪General Western Food≫
Grill Isomura
   1,Sonezaki-shinchi,Kita-ku   Tel.(06)345-1370

Imperial
   3,Dozima,Kita-ku   Tel.(06)458-1359
Hariju
   Dotonbori,Chuo-ku   Tel.(06)211-2980
Seifu Grill
   1,Tosabori,Nishi-ku   Tel.(06)441-3671
Rokuban
   Soemon-cho,Chuo-ku   Tel.(06)211-3456
Grill　Morita
   2,Nishi-tenma,Kita-ku   Tel.(06)364-8886

≪Okonomi-yaki≫
Tenma Kikusui
   4,Tenjin-bashi,Kita-ku   Tel.(06)351-6743
Boteju
   Dotonbori,Chuo-ku   Tel.(06)211-4478
Chibo
   Sennichimae,Chuo-ku   Tel.(06)643-0111

≪Udon-Nabe≫
Mimiu
   4,Hirano-machi,Chuo-ku   Tel.(06)231-5770
Nishiya Honten
   1,Shinsaibashi-suji,Chuo-ku   Tel.(06)241-9221

≪Udon≫
Matsubaya
   3,Minami-senba,Chuo-ku   Tel.(06)251-3339
Kanaizumi
   3,Umeda,Kita-ku   Tel.(06)344-5556

Imai
  1,Dotonbori,Chuo-ku   Tel.(06)211-0319
Kawafuku Honten
  1,Higashi-shinsaibashi,Chuo-ku   Tel.(06)241-9125

≪Soba≫
Yorokobian
  1,Dojima,Kita-ku   Tel.(06)341-1882
Hyotei
  2,Sonezaki,Kita-ku   Tel.(06)311-5041
Naniwa Soba
  1,Shinsaibashi-suji,Chuo-ku   Tel.(06)241-9201
Sohonke Sarashina
  Ebisu-higashi,Naniwa-ku   Tel.(06)643-1256

≪French Food≫
Chez Wada
  2,Nishi-shinsaibashi,Chuo-ku   Tel.(06)212-1780
Le Ponde Shell
  4,Kitahama-higashi,Chuo-ku   Tel.(06)947-0888
Bistro de Anju
  2,Shinsaibashi-suji,Chuo-ku   Tel.(06)213-8312

≪Thai Food≫
Sawadi
  1,Dotonbori,Chuo-ku   Tel.(06)212-2301
Chaitai
  2,Kouzu,Chuo-ku   Tel.(06)212-1324

≪German Food≫
Hamburg
  9,Tanimachi,Chuo-ku   Tel.(06)763-2370
Doitu
  2,Shinsaibashi-suji,Chuo-ku   Tel.(06)213-8545

≪Russian Food≫
Baikaru
  5,Namba,Chuo-ku   Tel.(06)644-5908

≪Korean Food≫
Tokyo Seikoen
  1,Sennichimae,Chou-ku   Tel.(06)211-2284
Tsuruichi Hontan
  5,Simoajihara-cho,Tennoji-ku   Tel.(06)771-0806
Souruchi
  4,Katsuyama-minami,Ikuno-ku Tel.(06)741-1605
Kannichikan
  2,Nishi-shinsaibashi,Chuo-ku Tel.(06)213-3089

≪Italian Food≫
Shirena
  6,Nozaki-cho,Kita-ku   Tel.(06)314-0813
Toritone
  1,Dojima,Kita-ku   Tel.(06)346-1712
Ristorante Parakuki
  4,Minami-senba,Chuo-ku   Tel.(06)282-0231
Holy Hokku
  5,Fukushima,Fukushima-ku   Tel.(06)453-4530

Ristorante Itaro
  1,Kyomachi-bori,Nishi-ku   Tel.(06)449-4847
Ristorante Vioretta
  2,Minami-senba,Chuo-ku   Tel.(06)263-0230
Ponte Vettkio
  1,Honmachi,Chuo-ku   Tel.(06)263-0677

≪Spanish Food≫
Elu Kaba
  1,Tosabori,Nishiku   Tel.(06)445-6679
Areguria
  9,Tanimachi,Chuo-ku   Tel.(06)764-1390

≪Indian Food≫
Ashoka
  1,Umeda,Kita-ku   Tel.(06)346-0333
Nabin
  1,Kyomachi-bori,Nishi-ku   Tel.(06)449-6789
Bonbei Kitchen
  1,Higashi-shinsaibashi,Chuo-ku   Tel.(06)245-9495

≪Pakistani,Arabian Food≫
Restaurant Taji
  2,Minami-honmachi,Chuo-ku   Tel.(06)262-0157

≪Indonesian Food≫
Dorian
  2,Kitahama,Chuo-ku   Tel.(06)229-9355

KOBE

≪General Western Food≫
Mon
  2,Kitanagasa-dori,Chuo-ku   Tel.(078)331-0372
Rengatei
  3,Kitanagasa-dori,Chuo-ku   Tel.(078)392-2941
Ito Grill
  1,Motomachi-dori,Chuo-ku   Tel.(078)331-2818

≪English Food≫
King's Arms
  4,Isobe-dori,Chuo-ku   Tel.(078)221-3774

≪French Food≫
Escargot
  1,Sannomiya-cho,Chuo-ku   Tel.(078)331-5034
Komushinowa
  4,Sakaemachi-dori,Chuo-ku   Tel.(078)361-7675

≪Indian Food≫
Delhi
  3,Nakayamate-dori,Chuo-ku   Tel.(078)221-3333
Kamaru
  1,Motoyamakita-machi,Higashinada-ku   Tel.(078)413-8702

≪Italian Food≫
Ristorante Donnaloia
  2,Kano-cho,Chuo-ku   Tel.(078)261-9291
Pinnochio
  2,Nakayamate-dori,Chuo-ku   Tel.(078)331-3330

Taberuna del Oruso
   2,Yamamoto-dori,Chuo-ku   Tel.(078)261-2490
Berugen
   2,Yamamoto-dori,Chuo-ku   Tel.(078)241-6952

≪Spanish Food≫
Carmeb
   1,Kitanagasa-dori,Chuo-ku   Tel.(078)331-2228
Elle Pancho Kitano
   3,Kitano-cho,Chuo-ku   Tel.(078)241-1344

≪German Food≫
Rainranto
   1,Ikuta-cho,Chuo-ku   Tel.(078)221-3949

≪Russian Food≫
Bararaika
   1,Nakayamate-dori,Chuo-ku   Tel.(078)291-0022

≪Swiss Food≫
Swiss Share
   3,Kitano-cho,Chuo-ku   Tel.(078)221-4343

≪Mexican Food≫
Tifana
   1,Nakayamate-dori,Chuo-ku   Tel.(078)242-0043

KYOTO

≪Kaiseki Ryori≫

Tsutsui
Gion-machi,Higashiyama-ku   Tel.(075)533-3911

Kinmata
Miyuki-machi,Nakagyo-ku   Tel.(075)221-1039

Kitcho
Arashiyama,Ukyo-ku   Tel.(075)861-0025

Sakurada
Karasuma-bukoji-higashi,Shimogyo-ku   Tel.(075)371-2552

Ishida
Yamatooji-sanjyo,Higashiyama-ku   Tel.(075)525-1515

Nakamuraro
Gion-machi,Higashiyama-ku   Tel.(075)561-0016

Hyotei
Nanzenji,Sakyo-ku   Tel.(075)771-4116

Nishiki
Arashiyama,Ukyo-ku   Tel.(075)881-8888

Tankuma Honke
Kiyamachi-dori,Shimogyo-ku   Tel.(075)351-1645

Kodaiji-Yamato
Kodaiji,Higashiyama-ku   Tel.(075)541-9111

≪Shojin-style Food≫

Daitokuji Ikkyu
Daitokuji,Kita-ku   Tel.(075)493-0019

≪Saba Zushi≫

Izuu
Yasaka-shinchi,Higashiyama-ku   Tel.(075)561-0750

≪Udon≫
Gonbe
  Gion-machi,Higashiyama-ku   Tel.(075)561-3350

≪Soba≫
Sohonke Matsuba
  Shijo-ohashi,Higashiyama-ku   Tel.(075)561-1451
Honke Owariya
  Kurumaya-machi-dori,Nakagyo-ku   Tel.(075)231-3446
Daikokuya
  Kiyamachi-takoyakushi   nishi,Nakagyo-ku Tel.(075)221-2818

≪Turtle≫
Daiichi
  Shimochouja-machi-dori   senbonnishi,Kamigyo-ku
                                           Tel.(075)461-1775

≪Torinabe≫
Hachikian
  Kawabata-dori   marutamachi,Sakyo-ku   Tel.(075)761-5470

≪Tofu≫
Okutan
  Nanzenji,Sakyo-ku   Tel.(075)771-8709
Junsei
  Nanzenji,Sakyo-ku   Tel.(075)761-2311

≪Fish≫
Heihachi Chaya
  Yamabana,Kawagishi-cho,   Sakyo-ku   Tel.(075)781-5008

≪Sukiyaki≫
Mishimatei
Tera-machi-dori　sanjyo,Nakagyo-ku　　Tel.(075)221-0003
Kimura Sukiyaki-ten
Tera-machi-dori　shijyo,Nakagyo-ku　　Tel.(075)221-0506
Iroha Honten
Pontocho-dori　shijyo,Nakagyo-ku　　Tel.(075)221-3334
Ichijyoji Junidanya
Ichijyoji,Sakyo-ku　　Tel.(075)701-7788

≪Tempura≫
Yoshikawa
Tomikoji-dori　oike,Nakagyo-ku　　Tel.(075)221-5544
Takasebune
Nishikiya-machi-dori　shijyo,Shimogyo-ku Tel.(075)351-4032

≪Bamboo-shoot Food≫
Kinsuitei
Shijyo-karasuma,Nakagyo-ku　　Tel.(075)255-5858

≪General Western Food≫
Manyoken
Shijyo-fuyamachi,Nakagyo-ku　　Tel.(075)221-1022
Kaiyotei
Ponto-cho-dori　shijyo,Nakagyo-ku　　Tel.(075)221-3607

HOIKUSHA COLOR BOOKS

ENGLISH EDITIONS

Book Size 4″×6″

COLORED ILLUSTRATIONS FOR NATURALISTS

Text in Japanese, with index in Lation or English.

Book Size 6″ × 8″

BUTTERFLIES of JAPAN

INSECTS of JAPAN vol.1

INSECTS of JAPAN vol.2

SHELLS of JAPAN vol.1

BIRDS of JAPAN

ROCKS

ECONOMIC MINERALS

HERBACEOUS PLANTS
of JAPAN vol.1

HERBACEOUS PLANTS
of JAPAN vol.2

HERBACEOUS PLANTS
of JAPAN vol.3

SEAWEEDS of JAPAN

TREES and SHRUBS
of JAPAN

MOTHS of JAPAN vol.1

MOTHS of JAPAN vol.2

SHELLS of JAPAN vol.2

FRUITS

ECONOMIC MINERALS vol.2

FRESHWATER FISHES
of JAPAN

GARDEN PLANTS of the
WORLD vol.1

GARDEN PLANTS of the
WORLD vol.2

GARDEN PLANTS of the
WORLD vol.3

GARDEN PLANTS of the
WORLD vol.4

GARDEN PLANTS of the
WORLD vol.5

THE FRESHWATER
PLANKTON of JAPAN

MEDICINAL PLANTS
of JAPAN

VEGETABLE CROPS
of JAPAN

SHELLS of the WORD vol.1

SHELLS of the WORD vol.2

THE MARINE
PLANKTON of JAPAN

EARLY STAGES of
JAPANESE MOTHS vol.1

EARLY STAGES of
JAPANESE MOTHS vol.2

FOSSILS

WOODY PLANTS of
JAPAN vol.1

WOODY PLANTS of
JAPAN vol.2

BRYOPHYTES of JAPAN

⟨NEW COLOR PICTURES⟩

Book Size 7″ × 10″

Guide to Seashore Animals of Japan with Color Pictures and Keys, Vol. I

Guide to Seashore Animals of Japan with Color Pictures and Keys, Vol. II

The Encyclopedia of Wakan-yaku (Traditionals Sino-Japanese Medicines) with Color Pictures Vol. I, II

Bird's Life in Japan with Color Pictures

Bird's of mountain, woodland and field

Bird's of marsh, shore and ocean